African |

Dictionary

Notebook with African Proverbs and Inspirational Quotes (7x10 Inches)

A J.D. Ware Production

This Notebook Belongs To:

_____

E-mail:

Phone:

InspirationalWares.com

Goals:

☐
☐
☐
☐
☐
☐
☐
☐
☐
☐

Accomplishments:

○ _____
○ _____
○ _____
○ _____
○ _____
○ _____
○ _____
○ _____
○ _____
○ _____

Habit Tracker	1	2	3	4	5	6	7	8	9	10

Appointments & Special Dates:

A small house will hold a hundred friends. ~ African proverb

He who learns, teaches. ~ Ethiopian proverb

To be without a friend is to be poor indeed. ~ Tanzanian proverb

To love the king is not bad, but a king who loves you is better. ~ Wolof proverb

Much wealth brings many enemies. – Swahili

However long the night, the dawn will break. ~ African proverb

A friend is someone you share the path with. ~ African proverb

He who earns calamity, eats it with his family. ~ African proverb

The wealth which enslaves the owner isn't wealth. ~ Yoruba

Show me your friend and I will show you your character. ~ African proverb

What you learn is what you die with. ~ African proverb

If you are filled with pride, then you will have no room for wisdom. ~ African proverb

An army of sheep led by a lion can defeat an army of lions led by a sheep. ~ Ghanaian proverb

You always learn a lot more when you lose than when you win. ~ African proverb

Greatness and beauty do not belong to the gods alone. ~ Nigerian Proverb

Wisdom is not like money to be tied up and hidden. ~ Akan

Patience is the mother of a beautiful child. ~ Bantu proverb

When the crocodile smiles, be extra careful. ~ African Proverb

No matter how the wild howls, the mountain cannot bow to it. ~ African Proverb

Peace is costly but it is worth the expense. ~ Kenyan proverb

Good words are food, bad words poison. ~ Malagasy Proverb

Even the colors of a chameleon are for survival not beauty. ~ African Proverb

Unity is strength, division is weakness. ~ Swahili proverb

Knowledge without wisdom is like water in the sand. ~ Guinean proverb

Ears that do not listen to advice, accompany the head when it is chopped off. ~ African Proverb

There can be no peace without understanding. ~ Senegalese proverb

Between true friends even water drunk together is sweet enough. ~ African proverb

When a king has good counselors, his reign is peaceful. ~ Ashanti proverb

What you help a child to love can be more important than what you help him to learn. ~ African proverb

He who loves money must labor. ~ Mauritania

Where there is love there is no darkness. ~ Burundian proverb

One cannot both feast and become rich. ~ Ashanti

There is no beauty but the beauty of action. ~ Moroccan Proverb

Poverty is slavery. ~ Somalia

If we stand tall it is because we stand on the backs of those who came before us. ~ African Proverb

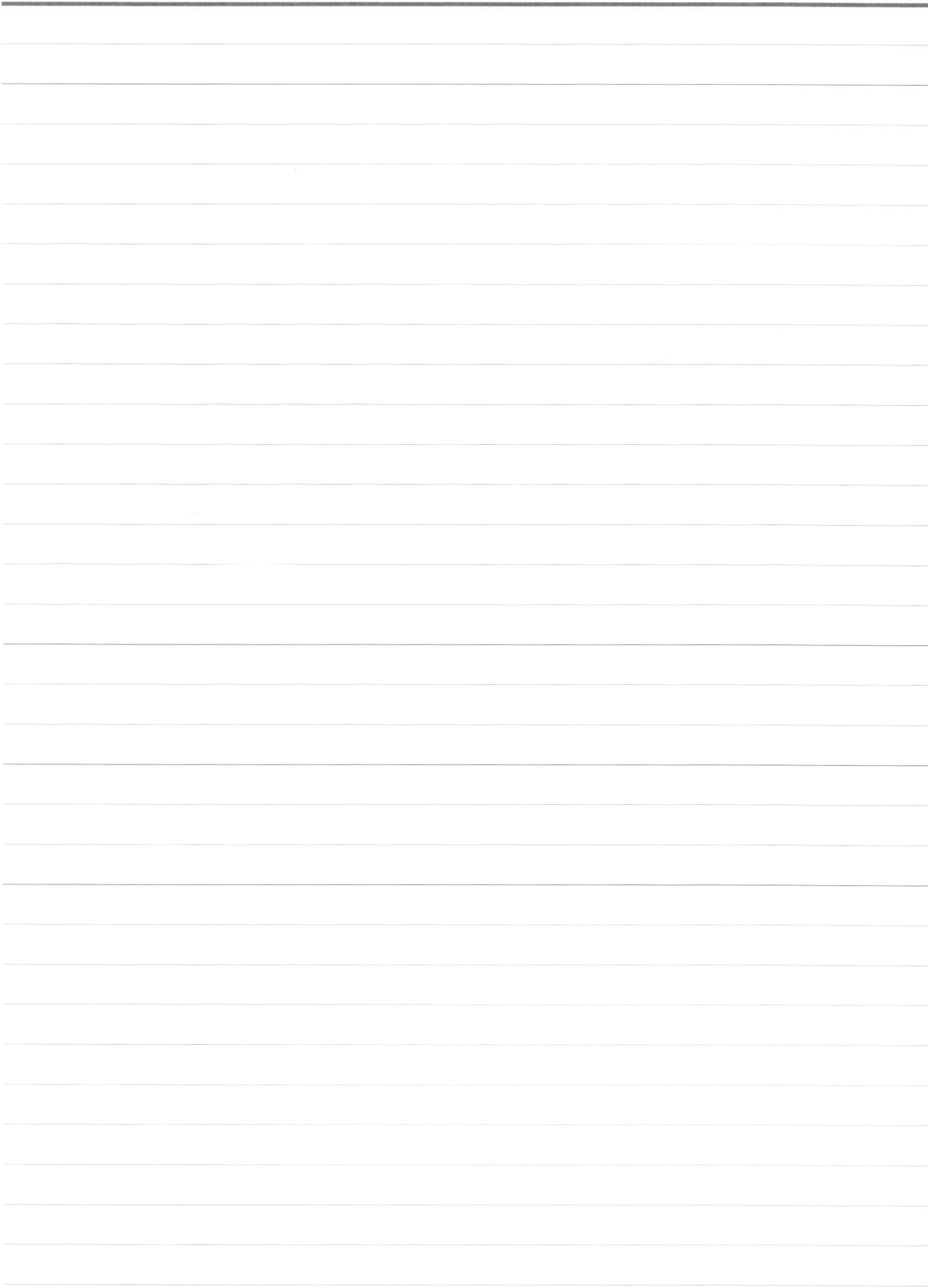

If you close your eyes to facts, you will learn through accidents. ~ African proverb

What one won't eat by itself, one will eat when mixed with other food. ~ Bantu & Lamba Proverb

The goat says: "Where there is blood, there is plenty of food." ~ Ghanaian Proverb

Wisdom is like a baobab tree; no one individual can embrace it. ~ Akan proverb

A family tie is like a tree, it can bend but it cannot break. ~ African proverb

Cooked food is not sold for goats. ~ Kikuyu Proverb

Nature gave us two cheeks instead of one to make it easier to eat hot food. ~ Ghanaian Proverb

It's those ugly caterpillars that turn into beautiful butterflies after seasons. ~ African Proverb

For more amazing journals and adult coloring books from J.D. Ware and Penelope Pewter, visit:

Amazon.com
CreateSpace.com
RWSquaredMedia.Wordpress.com

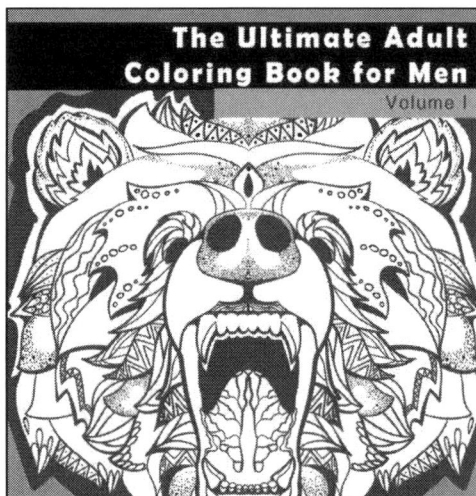

The Ultimate Adult
Coloring Book for Men

The Be A Pineapple Adult
Coloring Book

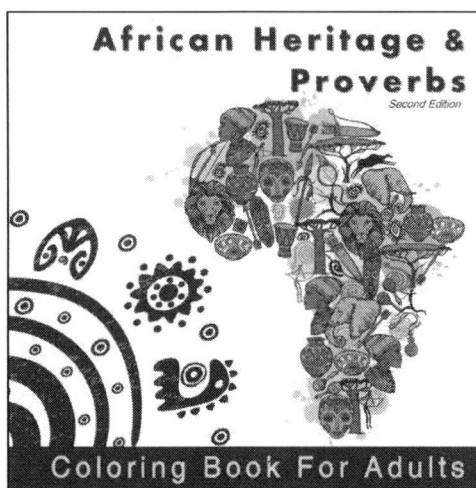

African Heritage & Proverbs
Coloring Book for Adults

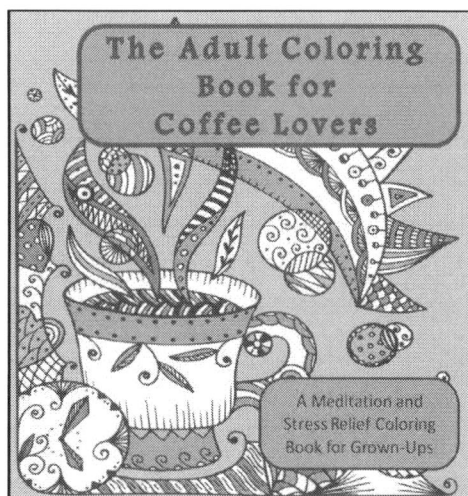

The Adult Coloring Book for
Coffee Lovers

InspirationalWares.com

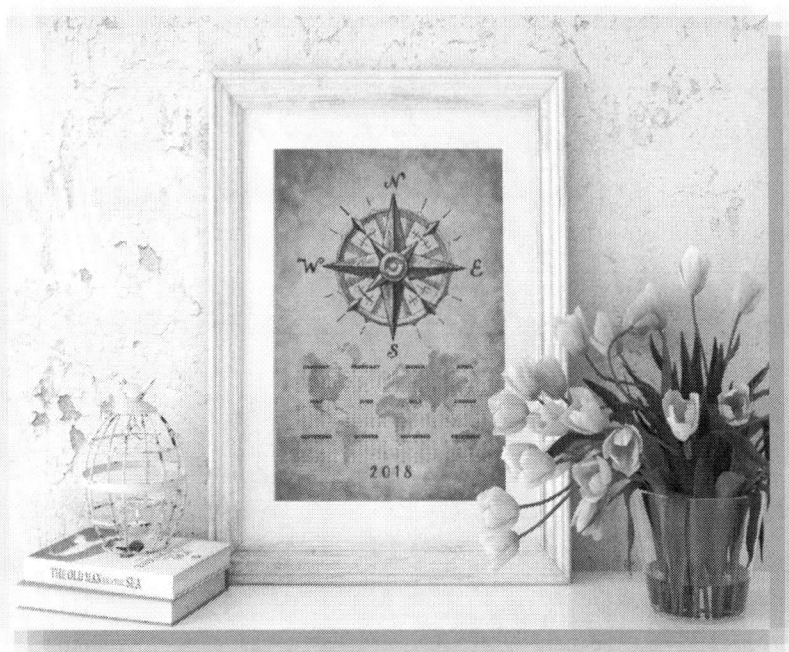

Funny & inspirational calendars, posters,
coffee mugs and more!

https://InspirationalWares.com

Printed in Great Britain
by Amazon